John de Bovilla

The quiet of the soul

John de Bovilla

The quiet of the soul

ISBN/EAN: 9783741112263

Manufactured in Europe, USA, Canada, Australia, Japa

Cover: Foto ©Lupo / pixelio.de

Manufactured and distributed by brebook publishing software
(www.brebook.com)

John de Bovilla

The quiet of the soul

THE

Quiet of the Soul.

BY

FATHER JOHN DE BOVILLA,

AN OBSERVANT FRIAR

OF THE ORDER OF S. FRANCIS.

TO WHICH IS ADDED,

Cure for Scruples,

BY

DOM : SCHRAM, O.S.B.

Edited by Rev. H. Collins.

London:

THOMAS RICHARDSON AND SONS;

26, PATERNOSTER ROW;

AND DERBY.

1876.

FOR ALL DEVOUT PERSONS.

————

I have found a great jewel; its great excellency consists in its being little. It is the wonder-working elixir, which the spiritual chymists, for many ages, have, with great industry, endeavoured to reach. But none were able to attain it in perfection, till this Reverend Author, by constant working in the furnace of God's love, hath, according to the true rules of art, prepared it for us. This Elixir is very safe, taken in whole or in any part, whereof a dram rightly applied, will cure any distemper. Be pleased to use it, and, upon your own experience, communicate it to others.

The Quiet of the Soul.

CHAPTER I.

Of the Heart and its Government.

GOD hath given to thee a very noble heart, made only to love Him, and, by His love, to be melted and consumed. Through love of Him thou shalt readily accomplish whatsoever thou wilt; and any difficulty shall be soon overcome through desire of virtue; whereas, if by thy own forces, thou attempt anything, thou wilt effect nothing. Let the intention of thy heart be well grounded, in such sort that thy outward working do spring from within.

And though penance and penal exercises be praiseworthy, when moderated with a discretion answerable to the condition of the persons by whom they are wrought, yet very often the best part of them do evaporate into vain complaisance, without any profit, and the toil is all lost, unless they be ruled and governed from within.

Man's life on earth is a continual warfare, as holy Job witnesseth. In this warfare thou must watch, and thy watching must consist in purifying and quieting thy spirit in all its motions. When any sudden storm

of passions and sensual unquietness ariseth in thy soul, be always ready with speed to settle
and pacify the same, in not grant-
ing it too much liberty to start
or wander out of the right way.

Do after this sort so often as
unquietness shall assault thee,
either in prayer or out of prayer.
Then shalt thou be able to pray
well, when in this manner thou
knowest how to work well. And
note that thou do this ever, not
with force or violence, but with
great mildness; for thy principal
exercise must be to quiet thy
soul and heart, not suffering that
they stray or be disordered, but
that always they be at rest.

CHAPTER II.

Of the Soul's care to settle herself in quietness.

WHEN thou hast attained to this good peace, thou shalt, without toil or travail, be led to great matters in much security, and shalt obey and suffer injuries without disturbance. But till thou art settled therein, thou must, for want of practice, herein sustain some labour. Nevertheless, thy soul shall be comforted in the contradictions that befall thee; and ever more and more thy spirit shall find greater quiet. But if at any time thou be so afflicted that thou canst not attain this quietness, then fly thou to prayer, after the example of our Saviour in the garden, and depart not from it, but persevere as did He, until thou find thy will conformable to God's Will, being pacified and reposed.

If thy mind or body be at some work or business, force not thyself to make a speedy finish of it, nor limit thyself to any time, in which it must be ended, but rather work the same sweetly in peace ; for thou must have God ever before thy eyes with great quietness, without all kind of respect of contenting any other besides Him. For if thou admit any mixture of other affections thou shalt soon perceive the

vexation and unquietness arising
in thy soul therefrom. When
thou risest from such falls, thou
wilt see how all thy hurt pro-
ceedeth from following thy own
humour. For when we endeavour that all things be done conformable to our own will, then
whatsoever falleth out otherwise,
doth afflict, trouble, and disquiet
us.

—✠—

CHAPTER III.

How this Dwelling of Peace is built by little and little.

SUFFER not thy mind to be
ever either lifted up or too
much cast down, but labour
always to preserve it in peace.

For our Lord saith : *Blessed are the peaceable.* Then will our Lord build in thy soul a house of pleasure. All that He requireth of thee is that, when thy passions raise thee up, thou shouldest sit down again, keeping thyself quiet in all thy works, thoughts, and emotions. But as a house is not built in one day, so thou must not think in one day to attain to this perfect peace and inward rest. And the Lord Himself it is that buildeth this house of peace. Without Him thou dost toil thyself in vain. But the foundation thereof is humility.

CHAPTER IV.

To obtain this quiet the Soul must be rid of all other comfort.

FOR to enter by this door of humility, thou must be earnest to embrace tribulations, and esteem them as thy sisters, and wish to be despised by all men, and that none do comfort thee but God. Let this be thy settled persuasion, that only God is thy whole joy, and that all other things be but thorns to thee. And think thou to thyself, that if thou wert led to some place, where thou shouldst receive some disgrace

and affront, yet thou wouldst go
willingly and with joy, being sure
that God is with thee. And fix
thyself firmly to wish and desire
no other honour than to do that .
that is for His honour and glory,
and to suffer for love of Him.
Thou must also force thyself to
be glad when any one wrongeth
thee with injurious words, and
despiseth or rebuketh thee; for,
under this rugged bark is a hid-
den treasure. Tribulation taken
in patience is a purging herb,
that scoureth out the dregs of
our imperfections and offences.
Moreover, to suffer with Christ
crucified is the only true glory;
but to follow one's own will and
desires, endeth in perdition.

When thy will desireth anything that seemeth holy, yet be not hasty, but submit all to God in great humility, beseeching of Him that His Will alone may be done in thee. And do thou acknowledge thy small forces, and how easily thou mayest be deceived under the appearance of good, by indiscreet zeal, which, like a false prophet, sheweth the look of a lamb, but is inwardly a ravening wolf. For whatsoever separateth the soul from humility, and leaveth her in vexation and unquietness, sheweth by its fruits that it is a wolf, and not a sheep. And so it falleth out, that what hath been gotten with much labour in many days, is in a very little while stolen away and vanished.

But if it chance thee to fall, be not troubled. Humble thyself only again before our Lord, and, acknowledging thy weakness, be advised against some other occasion. For mayhap, God permitted it so to fall out, to abate some secret pride, which is in thee, unknown to thyself. And if at any time some sparks of vice do touch thy soul, thou must not be disturbed, but sweetly draw thy spirit aside, and settle it in quietness, so as to be neither over joyful or heavy. Thus keep thou thy soul clean from sin in great peace, and thou shalt find God within thee, and shalt be assured that whatsoever He doeth, is for thy good and profit.

CHAPTER V.

How the Soul must be in solitude that God may work.

SEEING that thy soul is the temple of God, in which He doth lodge, do thou keep it void of all other things for Him alone. For alone He desireth to find thee, alone without thoughts—alone without desires —alone without thy own will. Seek not for crosses indiscreetly, without the counsel of thy ghostly father, but dispose thyself rather to suffer, for love of Him, whatsoever He may please, and how it shall please Him. Do not thy will, but let God's Will

be done in thee. Let thy will
be untied on all sides, so that
thou desire nothing. And if thou
desire any thing, yet so desire it,
that, if it take not effect, thou be
not therefore afflicted, but remain in good quiet as if thou
hadst not desired it at all. Then
shalt thou be free indeed.

God looketh to find thy soul
alone, free from the chains of
desires, which are a servitude,
that He may work in thee His
wonders. O holy solitariness!
O wilderness of joy, where we
may be alone with God. Take
off thy shoes and enter this holy
ground, O my soul! Salute no
one by the way. Let the dead
bury their dead, and fly thou to
repose in this land of the living.

CHAPTER VI.

That too great zeal for others hurteth this holy quiet.

WHEN God dwelleth in thy soul, He will fill thee with the love of Himself, and the love of thy neighbour. "*I came,*" saith our Lord, "*to kindle a fire on the earth.*" The love of God hath no limits; but the love of thy neighbour is to be moderated, lest it prove thy ruin. So must thou love thy neighbour as not to cast away thyself. Do not thy work for example to others, but do all things simply to please God. Think not that thy works can be of much benefit to others, seeing they profit thyself but little.

If thou wouldst have a thirst for souls, wait for it from God's hands, and think not to procure it by thine own diligence and indiscreet zeal. Keep thy soul in solitude, and loose on every side, till God bind thee to Himself. Wait in quiet of spirit till He come and hire thee into His vineyard. Strip thyself of all things that He may apparel thee with Himself. Having forgot thyself He will remember thee.

Be zealous, therefore, without disquiet, and let all thy works be done with tranquil soul. This silence crieth aloud, and by this want of all care all is provided, and procured. For what God desireth, is a soul wholly delivered to Himself, and separated from all other things. Being void of all else, He worketh perfectly in her all His holy Will.

———✠———

CHAPTER VII.

How the Soul is to surrender herself to God's working.

OUR Lord calleth thee to His quiet, when He saith : "*Come to Me, all ye that labour, and I will give you rest.*" And again : "*Ye that thirst come to the waters.*" This divine call thou must follow, but without hurry or violence, not running before the inspiration of the Holy Spirit, but waiting for Him to guide thee. By little and little, with sweetness and reverence, draw near with all thy powers to the Lord, lest by forcing thyself thou shouldest harden thy heart, and unfit thy soul for this holy repose. Bethink thee often of the goodness of God, and of His loving benefits, and the manner of His sweetness shall fall upon thy soul.

But beware thou procure thee no tears or sensible devotion, by forcing of thy heart; but wait on God, and when He pleaseth He will send thee tears, which shall flow with sweetness and peace without any force. Then mayest thou know with lowly heart that they are not thy own, but God's work in thee.

Know also that thou shalt suffer loss if thou depend any way on thyself. Rather then learn to sit thee down at the feet of our Lord like Mary, than to be busy with Martha. But when thou desirest to repose in God, see that thou limit Him not within the straitness of earthly comparisons; for He is above comparisons, an infinite immensity, and cannot be comprehended. He is everywhere, but He is especially in thy soul, for His delights are to be with the children of men; for though He hath no need of us, yet He hath made us worthy of Himself. He being found by thy understanding, let

thy will quietly and sweetly repose in Him.

In thy meditations or devo-
tions, task not thyself to any set
number, as though tied to so
much of reading or prayers, but
where thou findest repose there
rest to enjoy the sweetness of our
Lord when He is pleased to
communicate Himself. And
though it fall out that thou
dost omit what thou hast or-
dained to do, be not thou troubled thereat, but leave all without fear. For the tasting and
enjoying of God is the end
thou seekest, to which, when
thou hast attained, the means
thereunto are of no further use,
having now served their purpose.

There is nothing so contrary

to true quiet of soul as to tie oneself by force to finish this or that, whereby no freedom is given to God to lead the soul whither He will, but she is forced to go according to a man's own fancy and determination. Thus seeking God she runneth away from Him, for she preferreth to seek after her own way rather than to find Him and rest in Him after His Will. Wherefore, if thou desire to profit, attend not to any other thing than to find God ; and, when He is pleased to shew Himself, remain with Him, forgetting and slighting all else. But when He doth withdraw from thee, thou must again return to seek Him, by good exercises, until thou find Him : and when again thou hast found Him, omit and leave all else, finding true joy and quiet in Him.

Mark this point well, for many spiritual persons are cast away, and much endamaged, by being wearied out with their exercises, esteeming themselves to have done nothing, if they make not a full end of them. Thus they live after their own wills in bondage, never reaching the dwelling of our Lord, wherein alone perfect peace and quiet is to be found.

CHAPTER VIII.

Of Faith in the Holy Sacrament, and of offering oneself to God.

THOU must ever daily increase in thy soul the faith of the Holy Sacrament, seeing how our Lord abaseth Himself to exalt thee, and by His low estate worketh thy glory. Seek not that He shew Himself to thee in other sort than under this veil, for blessed are they that, having not seen, have yet believed.

Draw near, not to change Him into thy substance, but to be changed into Himself whom thou takest. Be ready for love of

Him to endure all pains and every evil, all dryness of mind and affliction. Remain firmly and steadfastly in Him, and when thou hast tasted of His peace and quiet, thou wilt find no content in any other thing.

---✠---

CHAPTER IX.

Comfort and delight to be sought only in God.

IF thou wouldst be perfect, make choice of afflictions and disgraces, being glad to be there where least friendship is shewed thee, and where thou art made subject. Rejoice when all

seem troublesome to thee, that
our Lord may have His will, and
be content, thou resting wholly
in Him.

But do thou nothing as of thy
own strength.   For though the
will of S. Peter to die for Christ
seemed firm and fixed, yet
being grounded only on himself
and not on grace, it stood not
steadfast.   To will a good thing
without leaning on the help of
God, is the beginning of a great
fall.   Keep thyself free on every
side, and determine not thyself
to anything till the time come
when thou must work it.   A
prudent care, however, that doth
not disquiet, is not forbidden in
the foresight of things necessary.
What thou doest, do it with dili-

gence speedily, but let thy soul desire nothing but God,—depending wholly on Him, and resting in Him.

Address all thy labours to thy Lord, and impart thy heart freely to Him. He will resolve thy doubts, and will lift thee up when thou shalt fall. He will absolve thee spiritually from thy offences, for He is an Eternal Priest, who, though He hath given power to S. Peter, yet hath not deprived Himself of the same. He will grant thee a jubilee as often as thou comest with perfect sorrow and entire love. If thou only lovest Him thou shalt want nothing.

CHAPTER X.

The Soul not to be dismayed at the sometime troubling of her quiet.

THOU shalt find sometimes, that, after all thy endeavours, thy soul is troubled, and the dust of unquietness is raised by the wind of thy passions. This our Lord alloweth for thy greater good. But a dew from heaven shall be sent to thee,—the dust shall be laid, and new flowers and fruits shall spring forth, by which thou mayest be made still more pleasing to His eyes. It was in these battles the Saints of God won their crowns. Whensoever thou art troubled do but say: "*O Lord, lo! here Thy servant. Thy Will be done in me. Do with me as Thou hast a mind. I stand wholly at Thy disposal.*" Blessed is the soul that in time of tribulation offereth herself in this manner as a sacrifice to God.

But if this battle do last, and thou canst not bend thyself to God's Will so soon as thou wouldest wish, be not therefore dismayed. It is thy cross, which Christ will have thee to carry after Him. Consider, if it please thee, the battle that Himself fought in the garden, when, as man, His weakness shrank, saying: "*Father, if it be possible, let this chalice pass from Me.*" But, presently, repairing this weakness, He meekly added: "*Yet Thy Will be done, not Mine.*" These be the labours and combats we must meet, after Christ our pattern, who did propose Himself as an example to us. Be not dismayed, though oftentimes thou long to be rid and free from these toils, but abide in prayer, until thou come to lose thy own will, and God's Will be fulfilled in thee. Labour thou that nothing but only God do lodge in thy soul, though for never so short a time. Let nothing be bitter to thee since all is from God. Look not either at other men's malices or faults, but pass through all things like a child, without irksomeness

or grief, neglecting all things but
God.

———✠———

CHAPTER XI.

Of the craft of the Devil to rob the Soul of this quiet, and how to escape his snares.

OUR adversary the devil goeth about seeking whom he
may devour. That he may
shift thee from thy humility, he
will seek that thou lay something
to thine own industry and endeavour, above that of others; whereby thou mayest come to despise
somebody or other in thy own
thoughts, as less disposed than

thou to receive God's gifts. This is the door of vanity and self-conceit. Be advised, then, and speedily pull thyself down, lest thou fall into the pride of the Pharisee. For if the proud fiend enter thy soul, he will soon, to thy great loss and damage, plant in it every kind of vice. For which cause our Lord saith: "*Watch and pray*," for both are needful to guard thy treasure.

Never let thy soul be in disquiet, for a peaceful soul worketh much and well, with great ease withstanding every hindrance; whereas, contrarywise, a troubled soul worketh but little and imperfectly, is soon wearied, and

suffereth an unprofitable martyrdom.

But to the end thou mayest
better look to thyself, and beware
of the craft of the devil, hold it
for certain that any thought
which causeth thee to have less
love of God, or less hope in
Him, is a messenger from hell.
For the devil goeth about to
breed fear in the soul, telling her
that her Confessions are imper-
fect, her Communions and prayers worthless, whereby distract-
fulness and alarm is raised in the
soul. Likewise, he procureth us
to take impatiently the want of
devotion or delight in prayer,
giving us to understand that our
labour is lost, and that it were
better to give over altogether

such barren labour; whereby fear and discomfort is increased, so that the soul thinketh herself forgotten of God. But all such fears are false, for the advantages springing from these drynesses and want of devotion, when borne in patience, are very great, if only the soul persevere in good works, nothing daunted. S. Gregory saith that the very patience of a soul in this bitterness is a prevailing prayer, and that her darkness shineth bright before our Lord.

It followeth herefrom that no good work is to be quitted, how destitute soever the soul may find herself of devotion; for the yielding would be to comply with what the devil would have.

The benefits to be procured by humble continuance in good works and prayers, that have no savour, shall be briefly put forward, that thou be not wholly disheartened through the want of all comfort.

—✠—

CHAPTER XII.

That great good cometh of dryness and temptations.

VERY great fruit may be gotten by spiritual dryness and the aforesaid indevotions, when borne with meekness. If thou didst but well understand this, thou wouldst not be so af-

3

flicted when in such case. But if
there were no' other consideration, this one might suffice, name-
ly, that such temptations do not
happen to great sinners, or to
such as are wholly addicted to
the world, but rather to God's
friends, and those who especially
apply themselves to His service,
separating themselves from all
occasions whereby they might
offend Him. Such temptations
are therefore not arguments of
God's disfavour towards us, but
rather of His love.

These temptations are like bitter medicine, very unsavoury,
yet withal very wholesome to
the soul, for they serve to purge
her, and to keep her humble.
But nature abhorreth the same,

and is loath to walk on the path of thorns and of crosses ; for the soul naturally esteemeth pleasure, and would esteem all that as lost labour that is not accompanied by delights.

—✠—

CHAPTER XIII.

How God sendeth temptations for our profit.

WE are by nature proud, and do easily presume more of ourselves than we are in effect. The very least savour of this self-estimation is able to hinder us from true perfection. Wherefore, our best friend and good Lord, that we may escape the danger, and be forced, as it were, to a true knowledge of ourselves, leaveth us to the trial of temptation. Saint Peter was suffered to deny his Master, that he might learn not to presume. God sent to S. Paul a temptation in the flesh, that seeing his own weakness, he might not be lifted up through the revelations given unto him.

Thus our Lord suffereth chosen souls to be tried by horrible and foul temptations, to humble them and make them careful. And that, which we think not profitable, worketh in His wisdom our greatest good. For, ordinarily, he who hath dryness of spirit, is persuaded that it is his own remissness, and that no true servant of God could have such a distempered soul, or serve God so coldly. Wherefore, by means of this medicine all high thoughts are brought down, and he thinketh himself unworthy of the name of a Christian, and the worst creature in the world. But to this humility of soul he would never have attained, but that he was forced thereto by his dryness, and by harassing temptations.

Again, the soul that is a prey to desolations and temptations, is forced to fly closer to God for succour, feeling that she would surely fall into some horrible sin, unless God interpose. Furthermore, in order to be rid of this martyrdom, she judgeth it expedient to eschew all kind of sin and every imperfection, and is spurred on to seek God with a whole heart, and to decline from all that is displeasing in any way to Him. These afflictions, too, are like a loving purgatory, cleansing the soul, and helping her, by patience and humility, to a greater crown of glory in heaven.

By all this may be understood what small reason hath the soul to be troubled, or to lose her peace, when made subject to drynesses and temptations. These things, far from coming from the devil, or being tokens of God's anger, are rather to be esteemed as presents of His love. All the soul must do at such times is to persevere humbly in her good works and prayers, though she feel no savour in them, accepting all as from the hands of a loving Father. Then, in the midst of darkness, the soul will be in quiet and in peace.

---✠---

CHAPTER XIV.

How the Soul must not be disquieted by her faults.

IF, at any time, thou fall into some offence or negligence, either in word or deed, such as to be angry, to murmur, to yield to curiosity, or to too much laughter, to suspect evil in others ; if thou offend once, or even fall often into the same fault, though thou resolve against it, be not therefore troubled, imagining that thou wilt never amend; thinking thou dost not force thyself as thou shouldst, which, if thou hadst done, thou wouldst not have fallen so often. Out of such broodings as these spring heaviness and distrust, and a despair of ever being rid of the said imperfections ; and so will confusion and shame invade thee, that thou shalt not dare to appear before thy Lord, as having carried thyself unloyally towards Him.

Some persons also would search curiously how long they

abode in their faults, whether they consented wittingly, and how far. And the more earnestly they apply themselves the less they discover, and the more are they filled with disquiet. Hence followeth also a great perplexity towards the confessing of their sins, to which they come with fear. And after having confessed, yet they attain not to quiet of spirit, for they will not believe themselves to have con-·fessed wholly and entirely. So they lead a miserable life, bitter and unquiet, disheartened from good works, and losing a great part of their labours. Such ought to content themselves with the opinion of some learned man, or their ghostly father.

If thou commit faults thou oughtest to turn with much confidence to the pardon of God, and not yield to a saddening of the mind. And this is to be understood, not only on occasion of lighter sins, but also of great offences; not only such as are committed by infirmity, but through malice even. This observation is most necessary for persons who wish to be rid of their miseries, and to make advance in virtue. And because many will not understand it so, they go forward without hope, downcast and dejected. They can hardly apply themselves to any good thoughts, so that they live a lamentable life, because they follow their own imagina-

tions, not hearkening to true and
wholesome doctrine.

———✠———

CHAPTER XV.

How a Soul is to quiet herself
without delay.

JF ever thou fall into a fault,
and if thou didst fall ever so
many times in a day, as soon
as thou seest thy guilt go
straightways to God, and, without disquiet, say to Him humbly:
O Lord, I have done like a
sinner, as I am, and nothing else
can be expected of me than these
and the like offences. And if
Thou hadst left me to myself, I

should have done much worse.
I am very sorry now for what I
have done. Pardon me, O Lord,
for Thy own Self's sake, and
give me grace not to offend
Thee again.

When thou hast done this lose
no more time in unquietness,
doubting that our Lord hath not
forgiven thee; but go forward in
peace with thy good works and
prayers, as if thou hadst committed no error at all. This
manner is to be followed when-
ever the fault is repeated, though
it were even a thousand times
done.

Much advantage is to be
reaped by this speedy return to
our loving Father, for thereby is
confidence and hope much in-

creased, and time is not lost in vain lamentations, which disquiet and dishearten the soul. This point is well worthy the study of those timorous persons who lose their time in scruples and anxieties to no profit, but rather to the ruin of their souls. For, if they only gave themselves up with confidence to this path of quiet, they would soon perceive the great spiritual profit to be gotten thereby; for by this means they would, in a little time, attain to great peace in the love of our Lord.

Let these counsels be read often by such, till they come to a full understanding of the excellent mystery. But for such as live carelessly, offending our

Lord by grievous sins, day by day, this remedy is to no purpose; nor is it intended but for such as seriously desire to make much progress in holiness of life.

Cure for Scruples.

A SCRUPLE is defined by Saint Antony to be a fearful fluctuation of mind, on account of certain weak and uncertain conjectures. If a man, treading on a cross formed of two straws lying on the ground, should, on the one hand, fear that he has sinned, but on the other it should seem that he has not, this anxious perturbation is a scruple. But they are utterly in error, who, if a man, through care for his salvation, and a filial love towards his God, examines

all his works, lest he should
chance to offend Him, pronounce
such an one scrupulous. This
man's conscience is to be called,
not scrupulous, but sensitive.
Scruples are sometimes about
the things of a man's past life:
for instance, whether he made
good confessions; whether his
previous examination of conscience was sufficient—whether
he omitted some circumstance;
whether his contrition and purpose of amendment, at the time
of confession, was sufficient, &c.,
&c. Sometimes scruples have
reference to the things of the
present. They chiefly consist in
the secret persuasion which scrupulous persons have, that they
are in a state of mortal sin, or in

their doing things with the fancy
that the things are mortal sins.
If some unlawful thing has met
their eye by chance, for an in-
stant, provoking them to evil,
then they doubt whether they
have consented. They fear
having cleaved to a bad thought:
—having given occasion for
some damage, either spiritual or
temporal, to their neighbour.
They doubt whether their indif-
ferent actions are not sins; whether they have been rightly bap-
tized, — are excommunicate, —
out of a state of grace; whether
they satisfy the precepts of the
Church, in fasting, hearing Mass,
reciting the Office, &c., &c.

Many evils and inconveniences
arise from scruples. (1.) Scru-

ples destroy peace and tranquil-
lity of mind.   (2.) They incapa-
citate often for the fulfilment of
the offices of Christian piety. (3.)
They generate wrong thoughts
of God's goodness.   (4.) They
bring on bodily diseases, and
sometimes lead to desperation
and madness.

The causes of scruples may be
divided into inward and outward.

The *inward* are: (1.) Igno-
rance of the distinct difference
between temptation and consent.
(2.) A secret pride and tenacious-
ness of the person's own judgment.   (3.) An excessive appre-
hension of the divine justice, and
too little confidence in God's
mercies.   (4.) An excessive
anxiety to flee all that has any

appearance of sin, and to have a
full certainty that this or that is
not sin. (5.) Too great austerity
and a sour dislike of conversing
with men.

The external causes are: (1.)
The permission of God: that the
good may be purged by spiritual
pains and may make progress;
that the *lukewarm* may become
more fervent in fulfilling offices
of Christian piety, and follow the
counsels of God; that *penitents*
may expiate their past sins.
(2.) Scruples may be excited by
the devil, to induce tepidity and
desperation. (3.) Conversation
with scrupulous persons upon
the matter of their scruples.
(4.) The reading of rigid books.

To these may be added: (1.) bodily causes, such as a cold, melancholy, or bilious temperament. (2.) A weak head.

From what has been said above, we may know the signs of a truly scrupulous person. They are: (1.) A pertinacious judgment. (2.) Frequent and trivially-grounded change of opinion, as well as inconstancy and tumult of action. (3.) Reflexions on numberless circumstances that are not of real moment. (4.) Fearfulness of committing sin in actions that are good. (5.) A ridiculous way of behaving generally. (6.) Perpetual fear about making a good confession.

Remedies for Scruples.

Contempt.—The Jews, from a
scrupulous observance of the
law, chose rather to be slain than
fight on the Sabbath day. But
considering the thing better, by
the counsel of the High Priest,
they determined to despise the
scruple and to fight. The faith-
ful, who scrupled to eat meat
which had been offered to idols,
Saint Paul exhorted to despise
the scruple, and to eat indiffer-
ently of all meat, if no scandal
was given thereby.

Prayer.—The prayer of the
scrupulous in temptation, should
be ejaculatory prayer to God, or

invocation of the Blessed Virgin and the Saints.

Mortification.—Discretion is to be used by a scrupulous person in mortifications, lest scruples be increased by the weakness of the head. But a soft life is often punished by God with scruples, that he who neglects the cross of mortification, may endure the more bitter one of scruples.

Purity of Conscience.—He who is knowingly unfaithful to God—displeasing Him by defects venially sinful, and by gross tepidity, and has his foot ever on the verge of mortal sin—he finds no rest in God, nor in created things; and not being generous with God, he falls into fears of grave sin where no fears should be.

Obedience to the Confessor.—S. Antoninus says: "They who refuse to trust themselves to the advice of superiors and prudent persons, in laying aside scruples, and acting in opposition to them, err many ways."

— ✠ —

Rational Scruples.

WHAT has hitherto been said about scruples, belongs to irrational scruples. Those scruples are not to be despised which are found to be rational. Saint Paul says, "abstain from every appearance of evil." Clement V., resolving certain doubts in the Rule of the Friars Minor,

says: " Oftentimes, where there
is not a fault, sensitive consciences fear one, for in the way
of God they fear whatsoever is
doubtful ; considering that in the
things which respect the salvation of the soul, in order to avoid
grievous remorses of conscience,
the safer side should be em-
braced." Rational scruples are
not then to be despised. They
are remorses of conscience, dis-
suading from sin, through faith,
the laws of God, or divine in-
spirations. There are consciences
to be found which are both scrupulous and lax. And if scruples
are to be easily despised, these
run the risk of despising grievous
sins. For such scrupulous persons are like the scribes and

pharisees, who strained at a gnat and swallowed a camel. Again, if all scruples are to be indiscriminately despised, there is a risk of confounding cautious persons with the scrupulous; a sensitive conscience with a scrupulous conscience. Thus, under colour of despising scruples, Christian perfection itself would be despised, which, rationally, is exceeding careful. The name of scrupulous is ill applied to those, who, from the love and fear of God, study, as far as is possible, to shun venial sins and imperfections. These are persons of a good and sensitive conscience, who follow out the counsels with filial love and quiet carefulness. Whereas, on the contrary, scru-

4

pulous persons are steeped in darkness, self-love, servile fear, and cowardly disquiets. They are tormented with scruples, because they only wish to avoid grievous sin. Those who study perfection are only persecuted by scruples to increase their merit, nor do they easily descend to what is lax, in despising things as scruples,

Rules.—The following rules are given for the treatment of rational scruples, which ought not to be despised,

1. When it is of little moment whether a thing be done this way or that, then, howsoever a too subtle scruple may cry against it, let a man, without further counsel or scrutiny, do

that which at the first look is represented to him as the good or the better thing.

2. When a thing is of some moment, either for the fulfilment of some slight precept of God, or for the promotion of perfection, then a rational scruple is to be listened to, and a consultation entered into, longer or shorter, according to the importance of the matter, till what we are bound to, or at least what is expedient, becomes sufficiently plain. So says S. Thomas; and S. Francis of Sales adds, that we should receive advice from the director of our conscience, applying also, if we please, to two or three men well versed in spiritual matters. For without con-

sultation it might easily happen
that a scruple would be despised,
which should not have been
despised, and that culpably so :
from which method of proceeding are generated ignorances
which do not excuse, **because**
they could be overcome.

3. This examination having
been gone through, if the scruple
still remain, and beget a prudent
fear, the "*perhaps I am mistak-
en,*" may thenceforward be held
in less esteem; when a con-
jectural or probable certitude
can alone be arrived at; or
when such a certitude should
not stand in the way of a prudent resolution concerning a
lawful thing : for instance, when
there is a doubt about being in a

state of grace, and of having sufficient dispositions for receiving the sacraments. For the sacraments are not to be passed by, because the unsatisfied mind says, " *Perhaps ·I am mistaken.*" Often, however, the scruple is not to be despised; that is, when it is for other reasons expedient to do what it dictates. And this is the case when the thing dictated, though not in itself obligatory, yet at least conduces to the more perfect observance of a precept, and a greater reverence for it. Indeed, to act against such a scruple can hardly be excused from venial sin, unless the perturbation of mind, or some other cause, should persuade to an opposite conclusion.

Take, for instance, if, on a fast day, a man were without cause to take a drink of chocolate, although a rational scruple, not to be despised, urged him not to do so.

4. Having made a previous examination as to what is most expedient, (a thing of less difficulty,) the more easy and profitable course, both for scrupulous persons and for others, is to choose at once what is most favourable to perfection, according to the saying of the Apostle, "All things are lawful for me, but all things are not expedient." To confirm this, Cornelius a Lapide alleges the saying of S. Clement, "They who do all they may lawfully do, easily fall into

doing what is not lawful." And Saint Gregory says, " He alone falls not into unlawful things, who sometimes cautiously refrains himself from things lawful." By this mode also the way to scruples is easily closed up, and to doubts too.

5. In the same fashion ought both scrupulous persons and others to take care, in their choice of opinion, to select that which most conduces to perfection. In doubtful things the safer side is to be taken. This, in a rational scruple especially, holds good with him who desires to please God as his best friend, —a most liberal Master—a most loving Spouse. Saint John of the Cross says: " If any one

would endeavour to persuade thee to some laxer doctrine, believe him not, though he should confirm it by miracles; but believe rather the doctrine of austerity, of penance, and of being stripped bare of all things.

Let a spiritual director take care to console a scrupulous person, but with great discretion, according to the counsel of Gerson. He should not be content with proceeding by the general and proverbial rules, nor with paying regard only to each particular thing, without respect to its principle; but he should carefully act from the consideration of both the one and the other. Nor should he be like an unskilful physician, who uses the same medicine for all diseases; but attending well to the circumstances, let him one while affirm and another while deny, doing so with sound reason; though this reason of the disparity of the cases seem scarcely apparent, just as in the Gospel we are taught both to manifest and not to manifest our good works before men. Now, as such skilful physicians are most rare, for together with learning there is required also long experience, it is not good indiscriminately to seek for solid counsel on questions of morality from every one. Nor ought all to presume to give advice, especially if they have not before them all the particular circumstances of the case, so as

to have it in its true form. The
director should treat a scrupulous person with great charity,
and again with great discretion.
In irrational scruples, the scruples are to be despised, but not
the person; but in those that
are rational a just judgment
ought to be formed of what is
lawful. According to Bellarmin,
any one wishing to be secure
about his salvation, ought by all
means to search out the real
truth, and if he cannot arrive at
a clear certainty, he should take
the safer side. The scrupulous
person should contend with tranquil mind after what is more perfect, despising vain phantoms,
but not despising sins, great or
little, not even the most minute.

A scrupulous person will find solid comfort, if, with humble docility, a serious desire to advance, and confidence in God, he seek for this consolation under a really good director. This consolation, however, is to be sought, not by emptying the heart altogether of fear, but by tempering fear with hope; not by despising all scruples, but by overcoming them through a zeal for advancement; not by an excessive dread of sin, but by placing alongside of it a love of pleasing God better. Nor does it excuse scrupulous persons, if they seek a director who does not care to bring them out of this state. S. Teresa complains of this connivance of directors who are only half good.

.But since, by our fault, or without our fault, it is not always in the power of a director to cure scruples, we must not be low in spirits, but bear our cross with resignation, which, though given for our own fault, is to be supported in hope till God provide.

RICHARDSON AND SONS, LONDON AND DERBY

www.ingramcontent.com/pod-product-compliance
Lightning Source LLC
Chambersburg PA
CBHW020242090426

42735CB00010B/1795